Awesome Stories of
GENEROSITY
in sports

BRAD HERZOG

"As shown by the wonderful stories in Count on Me: Sports, athletics can not only reveal character, but also inspire it."
—**Shannon Miller,** two-time Olympic gold medalist in gymnastics

"The true tales in Brad Herzog's books show how the games we play can teach seriously important life lessons."
—**Jake Delhomme,** former Super Bowl quarterback for the Carolina Panthers

free spirit
PUBLISHING®

Library of Congress Cataloging-in-Publication Data
Herzog, Brad.
  Awesome stories of generosity in sports / by Brad Herzog.
    pages cm. — (Count on me: Sports)
  Includes bibliographical references and index.
  Audience: Interest Level Ages: 8–13.
  ISBN 978-1-57542-477-4 — ISBN 1-57542-477-0   1. Athletes—Conduct of life—Juvenile literature. 2. Athletes—Charitable contributions—Juvenile literature. 3. Generosity—Juvenile literature. I. Title.
  GV706.3.H46 2014
  306.4'83—dc23
                                                                                            2014011048

Reading Level Grade 5; Interest Level Ages 8–13;
Fountas & Pinnell Guided Reading Level V

Edited by Alison Behnke
Cover and interior design by Michelle Lee Lagerroos

Cover photo credits: background © Bruxov | Dreamstime.com;
clockwise from top left: AP Photo; AP Photo/Emilio Morenatti; AP Photo/Sue Ogrocki;
AP Photo/John Raoux; AP Photo/Nathan Bilow; AP Photo/Greg Trott.
For interior photo credits, see page 102.

10 9 8 7 6 5 4 3 2 1
Printed in the United States of America
S18860614

Free Spirit Publishing Inc.
Minneapolis, MN
(612) 338-2068
help4kids@freespirit.com
www.freespirit.com

DEDICATION

To the always generous Horner family—Julie, Doug, and super swimmers Sedona and Delaney.

ACKNOWLEDGMENTS

Thank you to Judy Galbraith, Margie Lisovskis, and the rest of the crew at Free Spirit Publishing for having the courage to pursue a series of books celebrating stories of character in sports. I found Alison Behnke to be both insightful and inclusive as an editor, an author's dream combination, and Michelle Lee Lagerroos put in overtime making sure the designs were just right. Finally, I am grateful to Aimee Jackson for bringing me to Free Spirit in the first place and for her unwavering support and friendship.

CONTENTS

INTRODUCTION

Arthur Ashe was a world-class tennis player. In 1968, he became the first black man to win the U.S. Open. In 1975, he made history again by being the first black man to win Wimbledon. Yet he once said that if he were remembered *only* as a tennis player, he would consider himself a failure.

By that measure, Ashe definitely succeeded. He worked hard to fight social and political injustice beyond the tennis court. Today, U.S. Open matches are played at Arthur Ashe Stadium. It was named for Ashe not just because he was a great athlete, but because he was a great man.

Ashe formed many groups to work toward goals he cared about. For example, he set up the Athlete-Career Connection to help athletes after they finished college. He also started the National Junior Tennis League. It provides tennis and life skills to more than 250,000 young people each year. And he created Artists and Athletes Against Apartheid. This group protested the treatment of black people in South Africa.

In 1993, Ashe died of pneumonia. Even in his last days, he spoke against injustice. He protested the poor treatment of refugees from Haiti to the United States. Throughout Ashe's life, his philosophy was simple. As he saw it, "From what we get, we can make a living. What we give, however, makes a life."

That's what this book is about: People who have found joy in giving. These stories celebrate athletes and others who have used their success to achieve more important victories. Some have made a career out of a cause. Others have responded in a moment of need. After all, sometimes a single act of generosity can be powerful. For example, in April 2012, a young woman named Christina visited Florida's Daytona Beach. At the time, Christina was being treated for a brain tumor. She was in a wheelchair. When she went to the beach, Christina sat watching the waves. She wished she could get closer to the water. But it was very hard to move her wheelchair through the sand. Just then, six college athletes from New York came by. The men were in Florida on vacation. They offered to help Christina. Together they carried her wheelchair to the edge of the water and cheered as she dipped her toes into the ocean. The experience was a simple one. But simple acts of kindness can make lasting memories.

As the stories in these pages show, generosity comes in many forms. It can mean helping a single person, as in the story of the college baseball coach who donated an organ to one of his players. It can mean lifting the spirits of an entire town. That's what some undersized football players did when they brought big smiles to a tough-luck coal mining town. It can even mean changing the perspective of a whole country, like the disabled cyclist in Ghana who inspired his nation to care for all its citizens.

The generous people in this book gave in many ways. Each made a choice to do the right thing. And many were inspired by other kindhearted people before them. After all, Arthur Ashe's tennis talents gave him the chance to help many others. But the man who taught Ashe to play the game? That man was named Ronald Charity.

SENIOR PROMISES

2008 • DENVER, COLORADO, UNITED STATES

When Jeremy Bloom was 17 years old, he left the United States for the first time. As a member of the U.S. Ski Team, he traveled to Japan. He was excited to experience another culture. But his most lasting memory of the trip was from a simple bus ride. Bloom watched as an elderly woman boarded the crowded bus. To Bloom's surprise, other passengers got up from their seats. They cleared a path for the woman and made sure she was comfortable. Then everyone bowed to her. "I thought how amazing it would be if our culture gave them the same respect that so many other countries give to the oldest population," said Bloom.

So in 2008, Bloom started Wish of a Lifetime (WOL). This organization helps older people make lifelong wishes come true. Bloom's trip inspired him. But the skier was also inspired by his love and respect for two people. One was his grandmother, who had lived with him for the first 19 years of his life. The other was his grandfather. Bloom's grandfather had worked three jobs as a 12-year-old during the Great Depression. During World War II, he flew air missions. And later, he taught his grandson how to ski.

Bloom would become a two-time Olympic freestyle skier. He was a three-time world champion. Bloom was also an All-American football player. The athlete was able to make a lot of his own dreams come true. So he set out to help others do the same.

At first, Bloom wasn't sure if his organization would make a big difference or not. But soon he saw the power of Wish of a Lifetime. Bloom met a woman named Nancy Tarpin. She couldn't afford to visit her daughter, Lucille. Lucille had cancer. She was dying. Nancy just wanted to be able to say good-bye. So Bloom traveled with her to Arizona. There, Nancy and Lucille spent three precious days together. "It changed her life," Bloom said of Nancy. "And it had a profound impact on mine."

Since then, WOL has made hundreds of wishes come true. Many requests have been related to peoples' memories of their youth. Some memories were painful. For instance, Dorothy was a 75-year-old. She recalled a hurtful and humiliating experience from her childhood. Dorothy had grown up during the era of racial segregation. One day 67 years earlier, she hadn't been allowed to eat in a train's dining car. Black passengers were not allowed to share some spaces with white passengers. So WOL gave Dorothy a trip on Colorado's Royal Gorge scenic train. She enjoyed a meal and beautiful scenery, sitting with the other passengers as an equal.

Other memories were joyful. Bloom's foundation sent a 94-year-old man to France. He had met his wife

A WORLD OF DIFFERENCE

Wish of a Lifetime has allowed many people to see loved ones who live far away or to take memorable trips. But some older people can't travel. For example, Tom Burgett was in his seventies and had advanced lung disease. That made it impossible for him to travel the world. So instead, WOL brought the world to him. The group asked people around the globe to send Burgett postcards at his home in Alabama. Burgett figured maybe he would get a dozen postcards or so. But in the first week alone, nearly 400 postcards flooded in. They came from 44 states and 37 countries. "Words cannot express how much your cards have lifted Tom's spirits," his sister wrote to WOL. "Thank you from the bottom of my heart for making a wonderful difference in my brother's life."

there during World War II. In Paris, the couple renewed their wedding vows.

Bloom has also made it possible for people to publish their poetry, visit the Grand Canyon, tour a submarine, and ride in a hot air balloon. Other wishes are much smaller. "Sometimes the simplest things in the world mean the most," said Bloom. One 86-year-old man made the simplest request of all. He asked for a rug, so that his linoleum floor wouldn't hurt his feet. Bloom handed it to him personally. "This five-dollar rug meant the world to him," said Bloom. "But it wasn't just the rug. It was that somebody cared."

FOR THE KIDS

One of baseball's famous stories is about the great Babe
Ruth and Johnny Sylvester. Sylvester was 11 years old.
And he was very sick. According to the tale, Sylvester
received a baseball from the 1926 World Series. It was
signed by Ruth. The baseball star had written, "I'll
knock a homer for you in Wednesday's game." As it
turned out, Ruth hit *three* home runs that day.

More than 80 years later, Elliot Mast became a
modern-day, kid-sized Babe Ruth. Not as a slugger—
although he *was* an excellent power hitter. He played
for two youth travel baseball teams in Pennsylvania.
But Mast's similarities to Ruth went deeper. He
decided to hit home runs for sick kids, too. And he
started doing it at age 11.

Mast dreamed of being a major leaguer. But that
wasn't an option for him. When he was born in 1998,
one of his feet was turned the wrong way. Doctors told
Mast's parents that he might never walk properly. But

he had an operation on his foot at Children's Hospital of Pittsburgh. The surgery was a big success. Mast did more than walk. He eventually became a talented baseball player on youth teams in the Altoona area. He was a pitcher, catcher, and first baseman. As he put it, the hospital helped him go "from a cast to my cleats." So Mast decided to give back to the hospital the best way he knew how—through baseball.

Mast had noticed the work of Curtis Granderson, a New York Yankees outfielder. Granderson started a charity called Grand Kids Foundation. The group's goal is to give kids better education, and also to give them baseball opportunities. Granderson asked his fans to pledge money to Grand Kids for every home run, extra base hit, and run he scored. The idea inspired Mast. He contacted Children's Hospital and started his own project. He called it FTK: For the Kids. Mast described his mission as "playing for a purpose." As he put it, "I play for the hospital and the kids who can't play."

Mast dedicated his 2010 baseball season to Children's Hospital programs such as Child Life. It hosts events and provides toys, games, and books for young patients. Child Life works to make sure that kids' stay at the hospital is fun and, according to Mast, "not too scary." Mast pledged to donate $2 for every base hit he made, $5 for every strikeout he recorded as a pitcher, and $10 for every home run he hit. He also worked with the Altoona Curve, a local minor league team, to hold a fundraiser. He sold raffle tickets and collected objects to auction off, including jerseys and balls autographed by pro athletes. Mast used Facebook, Twitter, YouTube, and his own blog (elliotmast.blogspot.com) to spread the word. He also encouraged fellow kids to donate crafts to the hospital and become pen pals with patients there.

And all the while, Mast kept on slugging for the cause. By the end of 2010, he had raised his batting average to nearly .500. It was the young player's best performance yet. More important, Mast had raised over $5,000 for

Children's Hospital. In the following years, he matched or even beat that total. He also teamed up with a company called Phoenix Bats. They pledged to give 15 percent of the money they made from every bat to Children's Hospital of Pittsburgh.

"I want to do this throughout my baseball career," says Mast. "My goal is to inspire other players (of any sport) to think about others."

GOOD CATCH

During an Arizona Diamondbacks game in 2011, a player tossed the baseball into the stands toward two boys. One of them, Ian McMillan, caught the ball. At first, he raised his hands in triumph. But then he noticed the other, younger boy, who was sitting sadly a few rows in front of him. So McMillan walked up to him and handed him the ball. TV cameras at the stadium caught this act of kindness. "You, young man, are a star!" said one of the TV announcers. The announcers decided that McMillan deserved a souvenir, too. Later in the game, they gave him a bat autographed by his favorite player. The next day, the Diamondbacks gave McMillan another treasure—the chance to throw out the honorary first pitch. "If you do good things," McMillan declared, "good things will happen to you."

CHEERING A CHAMP

MAY 16, 2012 • WORTHINGTON, OHIO, UNITED STATES

You can show generosity by giving money to a good cause. You can also be generous with your time and energy. And sometimes, generosity can simply mean giving encouragement.

It was Field Day at Colonial Hills Elementary School. Everyone expected a typical 400-meter race.

Eight runners toed the starting line. Seven of them raced forward as soon as they heard the word "Go!" The eighth? He started, too—just a bit more slowly than the rest.

Matt Woodrum and his twin brother, Ray, almost died at birth. They were born three months early and weighed only two pounds apiece. Doctors were especially worried about Matt. They were afraid he might not even survive. One doctor told the twins' mother that if Matt lived, he might spend the rest of his life in a wheelchair.

Matt *did* live. And two months later, he was healthy enough to leave the hospital. Doctors had diagnosed him with cerebral palsy. The disease makes it hard for him to walk.

But on Field Day in 2012, Matt Woodrum decided to run. And he wanted to run a long way. The 11-year-old didn't *have* to enter the 400-meter event. It was the longest race of the day. Only a handful of his classmates even tried it. But Woodrum was determined. This determination was typical of him. He always tried to take part in every sport with his friends and his two brothers. "I have cerebral palsy, but that's not going to slow me down," he said later. "I really wanted to start that race, and I wanted to finish it, no matter how bad it hurt."

However, as Woodrum began his second lap around the track, he started to get tired. He slowed down—way down. He was almost walking rather than running. It looked like he might not be able to finish. Then gym teacher John Blaine joined him.

CYCLING FORWARD

Matt Woodrum's mother, Anne Curran, filmed his memorable 400-meter race. She posted the video online, and more than one million people have watched it. One viewer was Deb Buenaga from Delaware. Her son, Preston, was born with a rare disease. Preston faces some physical and mental challenges. To help him and other kids, the Buenaga family started a charity called Preston's March for Energy. It raises money to buy bicycles for children with special needs. Each cycle is designed specifically for its rider. Deb Buenaga was inspired by Woodrum's run. So she and her husband, Steve, drove all the way to Ohio. They presented a special three-wheeled bike to Woodrum. She told him, "I saw a video of you on television, and you were absolutely amazing."

Blaine jogged next to Woodrum as he struggled forward. Blaine urged him not to give up. "Matt, you're not going to stop, are you?" he said, encouragingly. "No way!" Woodrum answered. Blaine stayed beside Woodrum for the rest of the race.

And that's when something awesome happened. Woodrum's classmates began noticing how hard he was working to finish the race. They made their way toward him. First it was half a dozen students, and then a dozen. Soon it was 20. Then it was 30 . . . and then 40. They started cheering and clapping. "Let's go Matt! Let's go!"

Whenever Woodrum began to slow down, the cheers grew louder. Hearing the support, he would speed up again. As he rounded the final bend, it seemed as if the whole school was running with him. "Matt never gives up on anything that he sets out to do," said Blaine. The students "knew he would cross that finish line, and they wanted to be a part of it."

As his classmates raised their arms and shouted in triumph, Woodrum picked up his speed. He pushed on to the end. At the finish line, the joyful crowd surrounded him. "It was tiring, but it really helped when my classmates and my coach and everybody swarmed me," he said. "It was really encouraging."

Everybody who saw him could say the same thing.

YOU CAN PLAY

2011 • CANADA

In 2007, 19-year-old Brendan Burke told his older brother, Patrick, that he was gay. Soon afterward, Patrick felt the need to apologize to Brendan. He knew that gay slurs (mean remarks and name-calling) were common in sports locker rooms. And he knew that he had made some of those comments himself over the years. When he learned that his brother had quit his high school hockey team partly because of that kind of behavior, he felt terrible. "I said, 'I'm sorry if I made your life harder. I'm sorry if I ever made you think that because you're gay, I would love you any less.'"

In 2010, Brendan died in a car accident. Afterward, Patrick dedicated himself to fighting homophobia in sports. (Homophobia is prejudice against people who are gay, lesbian, bisexual, or transgender.) He had some important support. Brendan and Patrick's father, Brian Burke, was a big name in hockey. Brian was the Toronto Maple Leafs president. Together, Patrick and

17

his dad founded the You Can Play Project. The program's motto is "Gay athletes. Straight allies. Teaming up for respect." Patrick said, "We want to make locker rooms safe for all athletes, rather than places of fear, slurs, and bullying. The casual homophobia in sports has to change, so all athletes know that what counts is whether you can play the game."

STANDING UP AND SPEAKING OUT

Rugby and wrestling are tough sports. But it can be far tougher to be mistreated just for being you. Hudson Taylor and Ben Cohen decided to confront bullying and prejudice. Cohen is a former English rugby star. He created the Ben Cohen StandUp Foundation. This anti-bullying organization is aimed at helping the lesbian, gay, bisexual, and transgender communities. Taylor was a three-time All-American wrestler. In college, he earned national attention by wearing a sticker on his headgear. The sticker showed the logo of the Human Rights Campaign, a group supporting gay rights. Taylor later launched a program called Athlete Ally. This project asks athletes to sign pledges to help end homophobia in sports. "I might get teased a little bit, but I'm not risking as much as someone who is gay or being bullied," Taylor said. "It's so important that athletes speak out, because we have a lot of power."

Patrick believes there are many athletes who want to show that tolerance is a key part of teamwork. One of his project's missions was to get at least one player from every National Hockey League team to film a public service announcement. The announcement urged players to accept teammates "no matter who they are." Team captains, All-Stars, and former Olympians took part. "Everyone should have the same rights and freedom to play the game. Race or sexual orientation shouldn't matter," said Henrik Lundqvist of the New York Rangers.

Patrick also speaks to dozens of college and high school hockey teams. Inspired by his message, the University of Connecticut men's hockey team made two videos. The first was based on the project's main idea: "If you can play, you can play." The second video was a response to the project's Captain's Challenge. Each of the UConn team's four captains pledged to "encourage my teammates to speak up for each other when confronted with slurs of any sort."

Patrick's effort has also moved beyond hockey. For instance, more than two dozen sports figures from Duke University filmed their own public service announcement. The group included the athletic director, the head men's soccer coach, a wrestler, a rower, and a running back. Coaches and athletes from other universities have done the same. People involved range from UCLA hockey players to University of Denver gymnasts to George Washington University swimmers. They include figure skaters, basketball players, runners, and more.

Patrick will always feel sad that his brother's life ended just as he was starting to live it openly. But the You Can Play Project has brought him comfort. He knows that many athletes are tired of the image that the sports world isn't tolerant. "A lot of them are eager to prove that it is a more welcoming environment than people might expect," he says. Patrick also looks forward to the day when it isn't a big news story if sports figures reveal they are gay. Instead, he hopes for a time when "athletes are only judged by how they can help their teams."

A HOME RUN SPEECH

JULY 7, 1966 • COOPERSTOWN, NEW YORK, UNITED STATES

Sometimes a few words can show huge generosity. And sometimes, those words can make a lasting difference.

July 7 is a big date in baseball history. On July 7, 1948, Leroy "Satchel" Paige signed a contract with the Cleveland Indians. Paige had long been an excellent pitcher. He had been playing in the Negro Leagues.

These professional teams featured mostly black players. The league had some Hispanic players, too. At that time, Major League Baseball was only just beginning to allow minority players to compete. So the separate leagues existed until the 1950s.

When Paige signed his contract with Cleveland in 1948, he became the first black pitcher in the American League. At that point, he was already well past his 40th birthday. Some people thought the signing was just a publicity stunt. But Paige certainly proved himself that season. He even helped Cleveland win the World Series. "What a pitcher he was!" said the great Ted Williams. Williams knew this for himself. He once struck out against the oldest "rookie" in major league history.

And what a hitter Williams was! He said once that he wanted people to see him and say, "There goes the greatest hitter who ever lived." And Williams—nicknamed "Teddy Ballgame"—*was* great. In 1941, the Boston Red Sox slugger recorded a .406 batting average. This feat made him the last major leaguer to reach the .400 mark. Over his whole career, Williams batted an average of .344 and slugged 521 home runs. And he earned these impressive stats even though he missed parts of five seasons. At those times, he was busy flying dangerous missions during World War II and the Korean War.

But Williams wasn't the most beloved ballplayer. He could be cranky and strong-willed. He didn't always get along with sports writers. And in the very last at-bat of his career, he hit a home run. But he didn't even come out of the dugout to tip his cap to the hometown fans.

That's why some people wondered what would happen on July 7, 1966. It was exactly 18 years after Paige's major league debut. It was also the day Williams was inducted into the National Baseball Hall of Fame. People were curious about what Williams would say in his Hall of Fame speech. Would he lash out at the writers? Would he come across as self-centered?

Instead, Williams did the opposite. He graciously thanked the writers who voted for him. He also said thank you to the many people who helped him during his career. Then he went further. This day was a time when the baseball world was supposed to be celebrating him. Yet he decided to shine the spotlight on others. Williams turned the attention to the great players of the Negro Leagues, like Paige and home-run-hitting catcher Josh Gibson. Williams said, "I hope that one day Satchel Paige and Josh Gibson will be voted into the Hall of Fame as symbols of the great Negro players who are not here only because they weren't given a chance."

ROCKING THE HALL OF FAME

Geddy Lee is the lead singer of the Canadian rock band Rush. He might not seem like a typical fan of America's national pastime. But Lee has long been a baseball fanatic. Over the years, he has collected dozens of valuable autographed balls. In 2007, Lee visited the Negro Leagues Baseball Museum in Kansas City, Missouri. "I was just so impressed and so emotional about the stories this museum tells," he said. So he decided to purchase a collection of nearly 200 baseballs signed by former Negro Leagues players. The autographs included those of Hall of Famers such as Hank Aaron, Willie Mays, and Josh Gibson. And then, in 2008, he promptly gave the collection to the Negro Leagues Museum. It was one of the largest donations the museum has ever received.

This part of Williams's speech was only 36 words. But it stood out. And people remembered it. Williams was a war hero and baseball hero. Yet he later called that line of his speech "one of the things I'm pretty proud of." Soon, the Hall of Fame faced increased pressure. Fans urged the Hall to honor the great players who had been barred from the major leagues because of the color of their skin. And once again, July 7 became an important date. Exactly five years after Williams gave his speech, baseball commissioner Bowie Kuhn made a big announcement. He said that Negro Leagues players could be fully included in the Hall of Fame. Satchel Paige was the first one elected. Josh Gibson went in the following year.

RECEIVERS GIVE BACK

MARCH 2012 • ETHIOPIA

In the summer of 2011, NFL wide receiver Anquan Boldin was watching the news. He saw reports of a food crisis in the East African nation of Ethiopia. The area had been going through a long drought—an extreme shortage of rain. Crops and farm animals died. Famine (a severe lack of food) affected millions of people.

Boldin was a standout player for the Baltimore Ravens, who play in Maryland. Ethiopia is thousands of miles from Baltimore. But that summer, Boldin decided distance didn't matter. He wanted to help.

Boldin had long been pursuing good causes. During his second year in the NFL, he started his Q81 Foundation. It gives underprivileged kids more opportunities and better education. With Q81, Boldin planned events like an annual holiday shopping spree with 200 kids. Boldin says, "I didn't get to where I am by myself. I had a lot of people helping me along the way." Boldin himself grew up poor in southern Florida. "So I feel that it's only right that I help others."

A.J. AND A.J.

A.J. McCarron was a star quarterback at the University of Alabama. One day in 2012, he was driving home from practice when he spotted a man about his age. His name was A.J., too—A.J. Starr. He'd been at the football practice, watching his favorite team. Starr has cerebral palsy. That makes it hard for him to move quickly. So he'd missed the bus home. Now he was walking in the rain. McCarron offered Starr a ride. On the way, the two of them talked about football. The quarterback was impressed by Starr's love of the game. Afterward, McCarron told one of the Alabama team's directors about Starr. McCarron asked, "Can we get him a job here?" So A.J. Starr became a volunteer member of the equipment staff. That year he spent home games and practices by the field, helping out and watching his new pal A.J. McCarron throw passes.

As Boldin learned more about the situation in East Africa, he knew he couldn't tackle that by himself, either. The famine was affecting 13 million people in three countries. So Boldin decided it was time for an international effort. He teamed up with Oxfam America, a relief and development organization that gives aid and support to communities around the globe.

Boldin also turned to a friend and former teammate, All-Pro Arizona Cardinals receiver Larry Fitzgerald. He asked Fitzgerald to join him in shining a light on the issue. They filmed a public service announcement and started a fundraising campaign. Their goal was to use the money to buy wells, farm animals, and tools for Ethiopian villagers. Fitzgerald said, "We hope to energize our fans and the public to do what they can to assist."

Boldin and Fitzgerald decided that visiting the region themselves would be a great way to help the cause. So in March 2012, they took a four-day trip to Ethiopia. On their first day in the country, they joined local people who were building a wall. Many men and women had walked three hours to get there. They were paid very little money to lift and move heavy rocks all day. One of the men Boldin met had eight children and earned only $60 a year. "I know what it's like to do without, but nothing like this," said Boldin.

In Ethiopia, the two football players gave their support, their help, and their strength. They visited an agricultural school that Oxfam supported. They talked to women about their rights in the community. And they went to a livestock market, where each man purchased a cow for a village. "It's a way of improving life for them," said Boldin. "I don't want to be just another guy who played in the NFL. We have a bigger purpose to touch lives, and I'm trying to do that."

PLAYING ON

The girls on the Cypress Cyclones soccer team were disappointed. They were an under-10 team in the American Youth Soccer Organization (AYSO). The Cyclones had just played in the regional playoffs. They had lost 3–2 to the Huntington Park American Eagles. That meant that they'd also lost out on a chance at the state tournament.

But to the Cyclones' surprise, the Eagles players were teary-eyed, too. Most of the Huntington Park players came from a poor part of the Los Angeles area. The state tournament was in Davis, California—a long way north. The team couldn't afford the $3,000 they needed for the trip.

League officials told the Cypress team to be ready to take Huntington Park's place. At first, the girls were excited about the opportunity. What young soccer players wouldn't be? But Cyclones coach Bernadette Arizmendi saw a different opportunity. She thought about the other team's problem. And she thought to herself, "We have to help them go."

Arizmendi convinced her players that her plan was the right thing to do. "They won, and they beat us fair and square," explained Samantha Brown, a Cyclones player. "So they should be the ones who should go." The Cyclones decided to help make that happen. Arizmendi reached out to organizations that she thought could help. She contacted everyone from local radio stations to professional soccer teams to shoe companies. Meanwhile, the players' parents asked local businesses for donations. The kids started writing letters. "We emailed everyone we knew and asked them to pass it on," said Arizmendi. "The support was wonderful. It was such a great learning experience for all these girls."

One of the emails reached a celebrity—*American Idol* host Ryan Seacrest. He called Arizmendi and Huntington Park coach Maria Espinoza during his national radio program. In that call, he told them that the American Eagles were, indeed, going to the state tournament. Seacrest donated $1,000 himself. In addition, the Los Angeles Sol, a women's professional soccer team, rented a private bus. The L.A. Sol also booked hotel rooms for the Eagles. The Huntington Park players were thrilled. They returned from Davis as the runners-up.

Afterward, Arizmendi made sure each of her players had a pen pal on the other team. Plus, the Eagles and the Cyclones were invited to see a Sol soccer game together. They even got to meet the Sol players on the field beforehand. Because of an act of generosity, two teams that had once been opponents were bonded in friendship.

A few weeks later, tragedy struck. The Cyclones' assistant coach, Hugo Bustamante, whose daughter was on the team, was killed. The girls were devastated. Bustamante had been the team's heart and soul. "He would always tell us to keep going," said Samantha Brown. But without him, the team wasn't sure it *could* go on.

However, as the girls had already learned, support from others can make a big difference. At the funeral home, the Cyclones players paid their last respects to their beloved coach. Then they looked over their shoulders. Walking through the door—wearing their uniforms and carrying flowers—were the American Eagles players. Both squads had been there in each other's time of need. That generosity helped the Cyclones carry on and keep playing the game they loved.

A CHANCE TO PLAY

After Hugo Bustamante's death, the Cypress Cyclones made sure that he and his family would be remembered. The team worked with members of the Los Angeles Sol to hold a benefit game. The money they raised went into a scholarship fund for Bustamante's two children. Later, the AYSO started a national scholarship fund in Bustamante's name. Donations to the fund pay for registration fees and uniforms for youth soccer players. The goal is to make sure that every child has a chance to play the game.

A COACH WHO CARES

FEBRUARY 7, 2011 • ATLANTA, GEORGIA, UNITED STATES

It was the time of year when star high school athletes across the country hold press conferences. They use these events to announce the colleges and universities they've chosen to play for. This looked like one of those scenes. Wake Forest University baseball caps rested on a table. Behind that table sat 42-year-old coach Tom Walter and 19-year-old freshman out-fielder Kevin Jordan. Cameras clicked. Reporters asked questions. And someone was saying, "It was obvious that this was the right thing to do from day one."

But this wasn't a player explaining why he had made his college choice. It was a coach describing why he had decided to sacrifice something for his player. And that something was his kidney.

Ten months earlier, Jordan had learned that he was very sick. He had a disease that prevented his kidneys from working properly. By the time he started at Wake Forest, he needed treatment every night in his dorm room. But he still practiced with the baseball team when he could.

Meanwhile, doctors were testing Jordan's family members. They hoped one of them would be a match for a kidney transplant. But none were. So Jordan's coach decided to get tested, too. As Walter put it, he simply wanted to give his player "a chance to be a college freshman." "I didn't ask," said Jordan. "He volunteered."

WISE WORDS

"You can't live a perfect day without doing something for someone who will never be able to repay you."

—**John Wooden, Hall of Fame college basketball coach**

Jordan's father, Keith, was incredibly grateful to Walter. But at the same time, he wasn't completely surprised. While his son decided whether to accept a scholarship from Wake Forest, Keith had focused on what kind of man would be coaching him. He did some research into Walter's background. Walter's previous coaching job had been at the University of New Orleans. In 2005, Hurricane Katrina devastated New Orleans. Walter's own house was in 12 feet of water. But Walter focused on making sure his players were okay. He helped them move to new homes. He even helped some who were thinking about going to other colleges. "A lot of coaches wouldn't have done that," said Keith.

So Jordan chose Wake Forest. The decision may have saved his life. On the first day of spring practice in 2011, Walter found out that he did qualify as a donor. He soon told his players that he would be donating a kidney to their teammate. At first, the response was a few seconds of stunned silence. Then the team burst into applause. "Tom Walter would do anything for one of his players or former players," said Steven Brooks, a Wake Forest outfielder. "It was only surprising because it was such a major surgery."

The operation took place at Atlanta's Emory University Hospital. Both the coach and the player recovered well. Walter did agree to take it easy for a while, though. He watched his team's first post-surgery practice from the stands. Later, he explained his act of generosity. "This has always been about the chance for Kevin to have a normal life," said Walter. "The day he gets back on the field will be a great day for all of us."

Eight months later, that day arrived when Jordan went back to batting practice. He threw the ball from his center field position. He even ran the fastest 60-yard sprint of anyone on the team. Walter called it "the best day of my coaching career—by far."

SETTING GOALS

1973 • CHICAGO, ILLINOIS, UNITED STATES

When he was 18 months old, Lex Tiahnybik had a bad case of the measles. The illness caused him to lose his hearing. Later, Lex felt sad or angry sometimes about being different from other kids. But he tried not to let it slow him down. And, growing up in Chicago, he found a passion—a love of hockey. Lex's father, Irv, knew Stan Mikita. Mikita was a hockey player for the Chicago Blackhawks. He spent 22 seasons with the team and scored 1,467 points. Eventually, Mikita's career earned him a spot in the National Hockey League Hall of Fame.

When Lex was young, his family went to many Blackhawks practices. Afterward, goaltender Glenn Hall would offer Lex tips. Meanwhile, Mikita offered up slap shots. Soon, Lex was playing on a youth team. He no longer felt isolated and frustrated by his hearing loss. "He could be one of the boys," said his father, "by being a good hockey player."

But then a new coach arrived. He had old-fashioned ideas. This new coach didn't want Lex around. He figured it was too much trouble to learn how to communicate with him. The other players began to tease and bully Lex.

Irv hated seeing his son suffer. And he thought of other kids, too. "I felt if Lex had this problem, countless other boys around the country probably had the same problem," he said. These kids "were really being denied a chance to play." So Irv decided to give them that chance. In 1973, he formed the American Hearing Impaired Hockey Association (AHIHA). And, along with his famous friend, he started the Stan Mikita Hockey School for the Hearing Impaired. The school offers a free weeklong summer camp. It began with just 31 players. Since then, hundreds of skaters from all over the United States have taken part.

The school's volunteers range from sign language interpreters to college coaches to pro players. In addition, many former AHIHA players (including Lex) have returned. They want to keep the generosity going into the next generation. Their students include beginners as well as college-level players. Some are good enough to compete on the U.S. hockey team in the Deaflympics. This event has taken place every four years since 1924. At camp, the highlight of the week is the annual benefit game. It's a showdown between the AHIHA Varsity Squad and Mikita's All-Stars, a team of former NHL standouts.

Throughout the camp and its events, students are excited about learning. Gene Ubriaco, a former NHL player, has been a volunteer coach at the camp since the beginning. He appreciates how eager the kids are to gain knowledge and become better players. They "can't hear," Ubriaco said, "but they listen." Just as they do when playing hockey, the camp's students use their other senses to learn and to absorb information.

Back when Irv first talked to Mikita about the school, he didn't have any trouble convincing him to lend his name. Irv simply reminded Mikita of his childhood. Mikita was born in Czechoslovakia. He first arrived in Canada when he was eight years old, and he didn't speak English. That language barrier made life difficult. "I could hear the words," Mikita remembered, "but I had no idea what they meant." Most of the athletes at his hockey camp can't hear words at all. But they have realized that it is still possible to

RIGHT TO PLAY

Norwegian speed skater Johann Olav Koss is another star on the ice who gives back. In 1993, Koss visited the African nation of Eritrea. He saw children living in poverty and civil war. "I spent time with orphans who had their own dreams and were never going to have the chance to realize them," he said. "It motivated me to skate faster. Why should I waste my talent when I've been given all these opportunities?"

The next year, Koss won three gold medals at the Winter Olympics in Norway. He donated $25,000 in prize money to an organization called Olympic Aid. The group is now called Right to Play. It uses sports to educate kids and to give them hope, even in parts of the world where life is very hard. Nearly 14,000 volunteer coaches around the globe teach more than one million children each week. Koss is now the organization's president.

achieve goals—quite literally. The camp focuses on hockey skills. But it's really about teaching life skills to everyone involved.

Indeed, AHIHA also assists players outside the rink. Camp workers help kids get hearing aids, speech and language therapy, and more. Above all, the program helps them discover something about themselves: They can hold their own on the ice, so why not off it?

A GIFT FOR MOM

APRIL 27, 2006 • CELEBRATION, FLORIDA, UNITED STATES

Dakoda Dowd had a bright future in golf. As a junior golfer, she collected nearly 200 trophies. At 11 years old, she helped a local high school reach the 2004 Florida state championship. But by autumn 2005, something had changed. Dowd said, "My heart isn't in it as much as before." There was a clear reason: Her mother, Kelly Jo Dowd, was dying.

Kelly Jo had been treated for breast cancer a few years earlier. It seemed like she had beaten it. But the disease returned. It spread to her organs and bones. Doctors told Kelly Jo that she might only have a few more months to live.

Naturally, golf didn't feel so important to Dakoda anymore. However, she did tell a newspaper reporter that her dream was to someday play in a Ladies Professional Golf Association (LPGA) event. And it was her mother's dream to see her daughter do that—before it was too late.

Bobby Ginn was one of the people who read about the Dowd family. Ginn was president of Ginn Clubs & Resorts. One of his Florida resorts was about to host a new golf tournament. It would feature some of the world's best golfers. The company was allowed to offer spots in the tournament to two women who didn't officially qualify through playing. Right away, Ginn knew what to do. "Sometimes you hear about stories, but there is nothing one can do. This was a

A DRIVING CAUSE

Cristie Kerr and Morgan Pressel were both golf champions. And both had their lives turned upside down by cancer. Their mothers had breast cancer. Kerr's mother, Linda, has battled the disease since 2002. Pressel's mother, Kathryn, died in 2003. "We both felt helpless, and we don't like feeling helpless," they wrote in an essay for *USA Today*. "We want to do everything we can so others don't have that same feeling." So Kerr and Pressel became activists for the cause. They created foundations and golf tournaments to raise money. Together, they have raised millions of dollars. These funds go toward breast cancer awareness, detection, treatment, and research.

situation where we were able to do something," he said. He offered Dakoda a chance to play in the LPGA Ginn Open. "It's obviously a dream come true," Kelly Jo said at the time. "It gives Dakoda something to work toward, a goal, something to stay focused on. It's given me something, too, to get to the next step, to watch her."

When Dakoda played at the Ginn Open, she was just 24 days past her 13th birthday. At that time, she was the youngest player ever to compete in an LPGA event. She was nervous. But she had a plan. "I'm going to look over and see my mom smiling," she said. "That will take all the jitters away." Her plan must have worked. With a huge crowd watching, Dakoda birdied her very first hole. (A birdie is one shot under par.) In that first round, she shot an impressive 74. She even outscored several major champions.

Dakoda started the second round by pulling a club from her bag. The bag had the words "Best Friends" stitched on it. Above those words was a pink ribbon symbolizing breast cancer research. Dakoda chose her driver. Like all her clubs, it was inscribed with the letters KJ, for her mom. Club in hand, she hit the ball right down the middle of the fairway.

In the end, Dakoda recorded an 82. She didn't make the cut to play in the tournament's final two rounds. But Kelly Jo was proud of her daughter. "She made Mama's cut today," she said. And after Dakoda tapped in her final putt, tournament officials surprised her. They gave Dakoda a trophy similar to the one awarded to the winner. A message was etched into the glass. It read: "Your journey has inspired us all. Congratulations on realizing your dream."

Mother and daughter would only have 13 more months together. At the age of 42, Kelly Jo died. Her family was by her side. The next year, the winner of the Ginn Open received the Kelly Jo Dowd Trophy.

"THAT'S MY CHILD"

SEPTEMBER 2, 2012 • LONDON, ENGLAND

If you saw Oksana Masters in her boat, you might
not know that there was anything unusual about her.
Well, that's not quite true. You would know that the
23-year-old was an unusually talented rower. And if
you watched her compete in the 2012 Paralympics in
London, England, you might marvel at the courage

and drive that got her there. But if you only saw her from the waist up, you probably wouldn't know that she was missing her legs. Masters took part in the Paralympics along with her mixed-double sculls partner, Rob Jones. Like Masters, Jones is a double amputee.

Years earlier, Masters's success had started with one woman's generosity. That woman made a decision to embrace a girl who needed her. Nearly everyone else had abandoned that little girl.

In 1989, Masters was born in Ukraine. She was different from the moment she entered the world. Radiation from a nearby nuclear power plant had caused serious birth defects. Masters had six toes on each foot, five webbed fingers on each hand, and no thumbs. Her left leg was six inches shorter than her right leg. She was missing important bones in both legs. Sadly, her parents wanted nothing to do with her. Over the years, she went to several orphanages. Some workers at those orphanages abused her emotionally and physically.

So how does someone go from the depths of despair to representing the United States in international competition? How does a girl born so different become a star athlete? At the 2012 Paralympics, Masters and Jones won a bronze medal. Afterward, Masters described the key to their victory. She said that to succeed two people must row as one. "Your heartbeats need to match," she explained.

Perhaps that's also the best way to describe a moment, years earlier, when a generous stranger saw a picture of little Oksana. Gay Masters was a college professor. She lived thousands of miles away from Ukraine, in Buffalo, New York. And she wanted to adopt a child. Gay had hoped to adopt a newborn baby. But when she saw a photo of six-year-old Oksana, something clicked. Gay knew right away that the two of them were meant to be together. She whispered three simple words: "That's my child."

Gay brought the little girl back to New York. There, Oksana had several surgeries. Doctors moved one finger from each hand to where her thumbs should have been. Her left leg was amputated. Later, most of

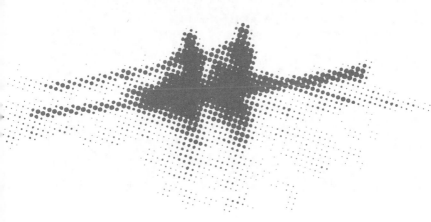

the right leg was removed, too. Doctors created artificial legs for Masters. Still, Buffalo's icy winters made walking especially hard. So Gay decided to move to Kentucky. If it was best for her daughter, it was best for her.

PROUD MARINE

Giving comes naturally to Oksana Masters's rowing partner, Rob Jones. Before he was an athlete, he was a U.S. Marine. He signed up for the Marines because, he says, "I realized there are things out there more important than me." In Afghanistan, an explosion damaged Jones's legs so badly that doctors had to amputate both of them.

Since Jones's surgery, many strangers have thanked him for his sacrifice. Sometimes they offer him money for a meal. Jones used to say no. But then he started saying yes—and using the money to help others. For example, he would take a $100 bill and use it to pay for a $25 meal. Then he would leave the rest of the money as a huge tip for the waiter or waitress. And when people have asked why he dreamed of winning a rowing medal at the Paralympics? Jones had a simple answer: Because it was his partner's dream. He wanted to give her that, too.

For much of her life, a lot of people had told Masters what she *couldn't* do. But when she was 13, she discovered rowing. It was very difficult to row well without lower-body muscles. But when Masters raced across the water, she felt calm and in control. Soon she met Jones, and they became a rowing team. Their success gave her confidence—in and out of the boat. For instance, she had been self-conscious about wearing shorts. But now she wears them often.

Masters also gained enough confidence to try another sport. In 2012, she started cross-country skiing. She took up this activity as a way to train for rowing. Then she fell in love with it. So at the 2014 Winter Paralympics in Sochi, Russia, she traded in her oars for ski poles. She won two medals—one bronze and one silver.

Many people have told Masters things like, "You're so brave." But she doesn't agree. "I'm not brave," she said. "I'm just living my life." It's a life she built with the help of two generous people—her mom and her rowing partner—whose heartbeats matched hers.

DRAFT CHOICE

JUNE 8, 2011 • ATHENS, GEORGIA, UNITED STATES

Zach Cone and Johnathan "J.T." Taylor were students at the University of Georgia. At first, they were rivals. As freshmen, they tried out for the same spot in the baseball team's outfield. By the time they were juniors, both were starters on the team. And they were also close friends. That friendship made what happened on March 6, 2011, even harder.

That day, Cone was playing left field. Taylor was in center field. When a batter on the other team hit a line drive between them, they raced toward each other. Both dove headfirst for the ball. Cone caught it, but the friends crashed into each other. For several moments, both of them lay still on the ground. Cone eventually wobbled to his feet. But Taylor didn't. He couldn't move.

Taylor had a serious spinal injury. Doctors said that he could not move his arms or legs anymore. Cone felt terrible. He visited Taylor in the hospital. As usual, Taylor tried to make *him* feel better. "This wasn't your fault, Zach," he said. "You just need to keep doing what you're doing. Don't worry about me. I'll be fine."

But Cone did worry. His coaches said he was good enough to be drafted by a major league team. Yet for a while he didn't feel like playing at all. In time, though, his injured friend and teammate inspired him. Even when the future looked dark, Taylor stayed optimistic. And he worked hard to get back some movement, little by little. "How is being bitter going to help me achieve my goals?" Taylor explained. "There are days I want to be sad, but I can't. Have to keep moving."

A few months later, Cone achieved one of *his* goals. The Texas Rangers chose him as a first-round draft pick. Cone was thrilled. But he was even happier after a Rangers scout called him with a question. The scout asked, "What do you think of the idea of the Rangers drafting J.T.?"

Taylor couldn't play baseball anymore. So why would a team draft him? As Rangers scout Ryan Coe put it, "This was a way to let him know that people are thinking about him."

Coe added that the Rangers' generous gesture was based on Taylor's talent. Taylor had been a great player—one the Rangers had hoped to draft all along. Before his injury, Taylor had recorded an impressive

PROFESSIONAL GESTURE

During a 2010 football game, Rutgers University defensive tackle Eric LeGrand crashed into another player. LeGrand's spinal cord was badly damaged, and he was paralyzed. Afterward, LeGrand became an inspiration to his teammates. The next year, he returned to the field on a snowy October day. As thousands of fans cheered, LeGrand rolled out in his motorized wheelchair. He led the Rutgers team onto the field before the game. A few months later, his college coach, Greg Schiano, took over as Tampa Bay Buccaneers head coach. Schiano decided to honor his former player. He signed LeGrand to a symbolic NFL contract. LeGrand announced that his #52 Bucs jersey would be sold online. He knew it would earn a healthy sum. But he didn't want the money for himself. Instead, it would go toward spinal cord research.

.312 batting average in 117 games at Georgia. "This wasn't done out of pity," Coe said. "As a baseball player he deserved to be drafted."

So, despite the fact that he might never walk again, Taylor was drafted in the 33rd round. Seven rounds later, the Houston Astros made a similar choice. They drafted top junior college pitcher Buddy Lamothe. The previous month, Lamothe had been paralyzed in a swimming accident.

In the end, Taylor decided not to sign a contract with Texas. He didn't want to risk his amateur status. He also wanted to continue his college studies. But on draft day, Cone and Taylor met in Taylor's hospital room. The two pals celebrated with Rangers hats on their heads. And that moment was priceless.

SOMETHING TO HOLD ONTO

JANUARY 18, 2012 • WRIGHTSVILLE, PENNSYLVANIA, UNITED STATES

Home fans don't celebrate visiting athletes very often. And in 2012, Abbey Rhodes was a visitor. She was a senior on the Hanover High School basketball team. Her team was coming to Eastern York High for a game. And Rhodes had no idea that her hosts were planning something special for her. But what goes around comes around.

The summer before her freshman year, Rhodes had surgery. It was an emergency operation to take out a tumor on her heart. Rhodes spent time in the hospital. She stayed in a unit for children with cancer. Rhodes watched as the kids there bravely battled the disease. After she left, the experience stayed with her. "I found out that I did not have cancer," Rhodes recalled. "I wanted to do something to help the kids that did."

So she decided to give young patients something to hold onto during tough times. Rhodes started an event called the Teddy Bear Toss. She asked fans to bring donations and stuffed animals to basketball games. The money goes to the Kimmel Cancer Center at Johns

Hopkins. The stuffed animals, which fans toss onto the court at halftime, go to an organization called Caitlin's Smiles. Caitlin's Smiles gives the toys to kids who have cancer and other serious diseases.

At the first Teddy Bear Toss, Rhodes collected 13 bags brimming with stuffed animals. Over her four years of high school, the program raised more than $5,000. It also gave more than 5,000 teddy bears to kids. It even extended beyond the school to places like the Lincoln Speedway in Abbottstown, Pennsylvania. The racetrack asked fans to bring stuffed animals to an auto race. The Teddy Bear Toss grew and grew. "Every year, it just got bigger and affected more and more peoples' lives," said Rhodes's teammate Shelby Barnes. "It just goes to show what one little thing can do."

Soon even more people noticed Rhodes's efforts. The local Red Cross gave her the Youth Community Impact Award. But the most unexpected honor came from a rival high school. In January 2011, Eastern York basketball player Bree Taylor was diagnosed with cancer. Rhodes heard the news on the day Hanover was supposed to travel to Eastern York for a game. So she arrived with a gift bag for Taylor. Amy Scerbo, Taylor's coach, said, "It kind of stuck in my heart."

One year later, Rhodes went back to Eastern York for another game. When she got there, a few things surprised her. Why was a television reporter there? Why was the crowd so big? Why was everyone from Eastern York wearing red shirts? And why did those shirts have a white bear on the front and "Bearing is 4 caring" written on the back?

Rhodes soon found out. Before the game, someone from Eastern York asked her to stand at mid-court.

BEAR BONANZA

Hanover High's Teddy Bear Toss is special because it was started by a high school freshman. But it isn't the only bear toss in the sports world. In fact, it has become a minor league hockey tradition. Each year, teams such as Pennsylvania's Hershey Bears and California's Bakersfield Condors hold the special event. Fans bring stuffed animals to the games. Then, after a player scores the first goal, the crowd tosses the animals onto the ice. Often, the hockey players personally deliver the treasures to patients in local hospitals. The biggest Bear Toss so far? In 2007, Canada's Calgary Hitmen collected 26,919 stuffed animals! It was a two-minute blizzard of bears.

The school had a teddy bear waiting for her there. What followed was a sort of thanks-for-giving parade. A stream of students and players brought in bear after bear after bear. Eventually, they filled five boxes and six large bags. "They just lined up," said Rhodes, "and kept coming."

Rhodes graduated five months later. But first, she found two younger students to continue the Teddy Bear Toss tradition. She became a student-athlete at nearby York College. She brought the Teddy Bear Toss there, too. Rhodes's dream is to work as a counselor for young cancer patients someday. After all, it was their determination that inspired hers.

LIFE GIVER

NOVEMBER 22, 2009 • PHILADELPHIA, PENNSYLVANIA, UNITED STATES

In the autumn of 2009, four women were fighting for their lives. Vicky Davis had diabetes and kidney failure. She was a 57-year-old mother of two. Alexis Sloan's heart couldn't pump on its own. So for more than two years, the 26-year-old had been constantly connected to a medical machine. Twenty-two-year-old Ashley Owens had been born with cystic fibrosis. This disease was causing her lungs to fill up with fluid. Every breath was difficult, and her lungs were barely working. She wrote good-bye letters to her family. And 25-year-old Meghan Kingsley, once a talented swimmer, had dozens of tumors in her brain and on her spine. She had tried an experimental drug treatment to shrink them. Instead, the drug had shut down her liver. She had only days to live.

Meanwhile, at a gym in Philadelphia, 25-year-old Francisco Rodriguez was fighting for a championship. As an amateur, Rodriguez had been a five-time Golden

Gloves boxing champion. He had gone on to win 14 of his first 16 professional bouts. That record had earned him a chance to win a title in the super bantamweight division. It was his first bout since becoming a father a few months earlier. His wife, Sonia, worried about his safety in the ring. "I'm always well prepared," Rodriguez told her. "Nothing is going to happen to me."

But something did happen—something terrible. In the 10th round, the referee stopped the fight. Rodriguez was losing. As he walked to his corner of the ring, Rodriguez suddenly collapsed. He was taken to a nearby hospital right away. He had three hours of surgery to try to stop swelling in his brain. But doctors couldn't save the young boxer. He slipped into a coma. Two nights later, Rodriguez was declared brain dead.

A few hours later, a representative from the Gift of Life Donor Program talked to Rodriguez's family. Would they consider donating Francisco's organs to people waiting for transplants? His organs could save lives. Sonia and Francisco's brother, Alex, talked it over. "I think you should give someone else a chance," said Alex, "now that he doesn't have one." Sonia agreed. She said, "He wanted to be a hero. He would always tell me that."

If that was Francisco Rodriguez's goal in life, Sonia and Alex decided, it would be his gift in death. Over the next two days, the fighter's organs gave others a fighting chance. As his brother puts it, Rodriguez "multiplied." Ashley Owens received his lungs. She soon discovered the joys of breathing deeply again. Meghan Kingsley received a liver transplant. Vicky Davis was given Rodriguez's kidneys and pancreas. And his heart went to Alexis Sloan—who happened to be a boxing fan from Philadelphia.

Four months later, Sonia Rodriguez got permission to write letters to the four women. She told them about her beloved husband. "I want to have them as part of my life," she says. "Through them, I feel like I'm going to be able to continue a relationship with Francisco. And I want them to have a relationship with my daughter, too," she continues. "One day they can also tell her how he changed their lives."

Later, the four women flew to Chicago. They had an emotional meeting with Rodriguez's family, including his baby daughter. They also met his uncle, who had received the boxer's other kidney. The family shared stories and photos of Rodriguez. Then the four women decided to visit the cemetery where he was buried. Alexis stood over his grave with tears flowing down her face. "You're my hero," she said. "I'm very proud to know that I have the heart of a champion."

WINTER WONDER

When Sonia Rodriguez donated her husband's organs, she turned his tragic death into a life-saving cause. A girl named Winter Vinecki is making a similar effort. In 2009, Vinecki's father died from prostate cancer. Ever since, she has dedicated herself to raising awareness about the disease. She does this by running. In 2012, Vinecki ran her first marathon. That first race was in Oregon. Within 18 months, she became the youngest person to finish marathons on all seven continents—even Antarctica! She was 14 years old at the time. As she explained, "These races weren't about me." But people paid attention to her races—and that helped her mission. Vinecki and her mother started an organization called Team Winter. It has raised more than $400,000 for prostate cancer research.

HOPE THROUGH HOOPS

2009 • NIGERIA

Mobolaji Akiode wasn't happy. She had spent her early childhood in her homeland of Nigeria. When she was eight years old, her family settled down in New Jersey. But Akiode just felt like she didn't belong. She was taller than other girls, and she spoke with an accent. Other students bullied her. Then, one day, things changed. That afternoon, some kids playing basketball noticed her standing nearby. "She's tall!" they said. "Come play." And for Akiode, basketball made all the difference.

"Participating in sports does so much for your confidence, especially at a young age," she said. "You get to socially network with other girls like you. You get to learn more. You get to build confidence." Akiode soon helped her high school team reach the 1998 state championship. She went on to star at Fordham

University. By the time she graduated, she was the school's eighth-best career scorer. In 2004, she even played for the Nigerian national basketball team in the Summer Olympics.

Later, Akiode got a job as an accountant for ESPN. She was living in Connecticut. But Nigeria was constantly on her mind. "I've used basketball as a tool to realize my greatest dreams," she said. "I didn't see enough opportunities put in place for more girls from Africa to have the same dream."

So Akiode decided to make those dreams possible. She left her job and moved back to Nigeria. Akiode has described Nigeria as "a society where boys are usually favored." She thinks this is true especially when it comes to sports. Parents often ask their young daughters to work to bring in extra money. That makes it hard for girls to even finish school, let alone find time for sports. "Nigeria is very behind on using sports as a social tool," says Akiode. "It recognizes the skills on the court, but it doesn't understand everything that goes along with it. Girls can feel as if they don't belong anywhere."

So Akiode made it her mission to use basketball to inspire Nigerian girls. She launched Hope4Girls (H4G). H4G uses basketball to create "an environment where the focus is on the girls," Akiode says. It's a place where "they can feel good about themselves."

WISE WORDS

"Getting started as a volunteer anywhere can be a challenge to a lot of people. The biggest hurdle is that people think they have to give all of their spare time. But if you only have a half hour, you can still make a difference."
—Jackie Joyner-Kersee, Olympic track and field gold medalist

To get started, Akiode began collecting small donations from friends and coworkers. With this money, she put together her first H4G sports camp. Sixty-five girls showed up. Some of them traveled for two or three days—by bus or on foot— just to take part. "They were so desperate for something like this. They were so hungry," said Akiode. As one camper put it, "I'm so excited. I have this joy in my spirit."

Akiode now lives fulltime in Nigeria. And Hope4Girls is going strong. It offers two main programs. One is the national camp, which happens once a year. The event brings together coaches and former players from the United States and Nigeria. Naturally, these experts teach the girls basketball. But they go further. They talk with them about important topics such as education and health. Some players have gone on to play in regional championships in Nigeria. Even those girls who don't continue to play basketball gain social skills and knowledge that help them in school and in life.

H4G's other program is the Princess Classic. This week-long basketball camp and tournament aims to increase sporting opportunities for girls at schools that don't have much money. The first guest host of the tournament was Yolanda Griffith. Griffith is a former MVP of the Women's National Basketball Association in the United States.

Akiode is proud of what she's done with Hope4Girls. "I expected to just give basketball and bring empowerment," she says. "What I got back was so much more." Akiode has gained motivation, inspiration, and joy from watching the girls at her camp learn and grow. Then again, as a traditional African proverb states, "What you give you get, ten times over."

SMALL WONDER

"The kids are so starry-eyed and excited. Quite a few of them couldn't even sleep the past few nights," said fourth-grade teacher Jack Spleen. Spleen taught at John S. Clarke Elementary School in Pottsville, Pennsylvania. As he spoke, a steady stream of football players stepped off a bus outside the school. It was a chilly day in late October. Local cheerleaders performed a routine. The whole town seemed to be gathered in anticipation. College teams from the Army and Navy military academies had come to this little town in eastern Pennsylvania to play a game. This was a big deal.

So . . . why were the players so small?

Most people have never heard of a college sport called sprint football. After all, there are only seven colleges and universities in the Collegiate Sprint Football League. The sport is exactly like regular college football. Well, almost exactly. The differences

73

include the facts that players aren't recruited, fans are few, and no player can weigh more than 172 pounds. That's right. It used to be called lightweight football. It's football for little guys.

Like sprint football, Pottsville was also often overlooked. It's a small town in Pennsylvania's coal mining region. Once, it had been home to an NFL team. The Pottsville Maroons were based there from 1925 to

SUITING UP FOR DANNY

Danny Keefe was born with differences. For example, he has a hard time speaking. But that hasn't stopped him from being part of the action. At six years old, he became the "official water coach" of the Bridgewater Badgers. They're a peewee football team in Danny's hometown of Bridgewater, Massachusetts. One day the Badgers noticed some kids at school picking on Danny. They decided to show him how much they cared about him. Danny is known for wearing a suit and tie every day. Some people made fun of that. The football players decided to give Danny their support by all wearing suits to school one day. They called it "Danny Appreciation Day." The team's gift of encouragement and friendship meant a lot to Danny. As his mother said, "he felt very loved."

1928. But decades later, it was home to people struggling to make ends meet. It was also home to many parents trying to find role models for their children. That's why the city's Joint Veterans Council decided to sponsor an annual sprint football game. Both the sport and the city deserved positive attention. And they could each give that attention to the other. Pottsville hosted the big game from 1983 to 2001.

Army coach Bob Thompson said his players were the type of young men who "got a lot of character and tough-guy awards" in high school. In 1993, that character was on display. The Army and Navy players generously gave their time and energy not just to playing the game, but to getting to know Pottsville's people. Members of both teams visited sick children in the local hospital and signed autographs for fans. They talked to students about the dangers of drugs and alcohol. They even took part in a pep rally featuring Navy's fight song, "Anchors Aweigh," played by a fourth-grade flutophone band.

In return, Pottsville residents opened their homes to the town's guests. The players didn't stay in hotels. Instead, they stayed in the homes of Pottsville residents. Players and hosts got to know each other. "For most of the guys on the team, it's like a second family," said Army linebacker James Lewis.

For the city, the game stood for community pride. For the players, it was a chance to shine. "To the kids," said Spleen, "seeing these athletes perform on the field is just as exciting as watching professional football players." Usually, on college campuses, only a few hundred fans would show up to sprint football games. And most of those fans were parents and friends. Yet on this autumn Saturday, 3,000 fans filled Veterans' Memorial Stadium at Pottsville High. That day, Army rolled to a 28–3 victory in a game known as the Anthracite Bowl.

What is anthracite, you ask? It is the blackest form of coal. It burns very hot. And it has a nickname that also describes the game that brought together athletes looking to shine and a town looking for heroes. They call it "buried sunshine."

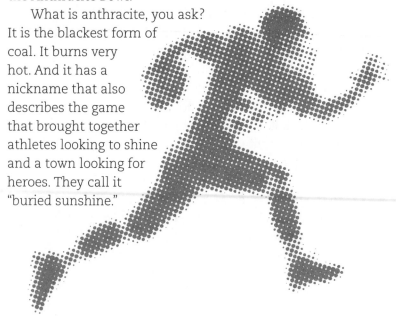

CARE AND COMFORT

2001 • GHANA

It was Christmas Eve, 1997. Emmanuel Ofosu Yeboah was in the African nation of Ghana. The 20-year-old sat by his mother's side. She was dying.

Yeboah's mother was by far the most important person in his life. She had always stood by him—even when others wouldn't. When Yeboah was born, his

right leg was severely deformed. In his culture, babies
with disabilities were sometimes left to die. Many children and adults who grew up with disabilities became
street beggars. Yeboah's father was ashamed of his
son. He left the family.

But Yeboah's mother, Comfort, refused to abandon
her child. Times were hard. Mother and son lived in a
tiny home without plumbing or electricity. But Yeboah
later said that his mom taught him an important
lesson. She told him that he "could go to school and
become a great man." In fact, Yeboah's mother carried
him two miles to school each day.

Just before Comfort died, she whispered a last
piece of wisdom to her son. He would carry these

words with him forever: "Don't let anyone put you
down because of your disability."

Inspired by those words, Yeboah decided to honor
his mother. And at the same time, he decided to lift
up his countrymen. He vowed to do it by riding a
bicycle—all the way across Ghana.

Yeboah had heard about an organization in
California called the Challenged Athletes Foundation
(CAF). It offers programs for disabled athletes. The
CAF also provides money for equipment, training,
and competition. Yeboah wrote a letter to the CAF. He
asked them for a bike. He said he would use it to raise
awareness about the struggles of Ghana's nearly two
million disabled residents. CAF cofounder Bob Babbitt
was moved by the simple request. So he sent a bike—
and more. He also gave Yeboah cycling gear and $1,000
to get his journey started. Babbitt admired Yeboah's
determination. "He never lets anybody define his lim-
its," he said.

In 2001, at age 24, Yeboah got on his bike. Over
the course of 10 days and nights, he used his one leg
to pedal 600 kilometers (380 miles). Across Ghana,
Yeboah talked with kids who had disabilities. He met
with village chiefs. He gave speeches and TV inter-
views. Everywhere, his message was the same: People
with physical challenges can do great things. They

can contribute to society. And they deserve as much respect as anyone else.

Along the way, he became an international celebrity. Nike gave him an award and a prize of $25,000. The CAF matched that amount. With this money, Yeboah created the Emmanuel Education Fund in Ghana. It pays for the schooling of 15 disabled students each year.

Yeboah's athletic journey didn't end with his bike ride. After getting an artificial leg, he became an excellent triathlete and soccer player. He also continues to give back. He has given hundreds of wheelchairs to people in need throughout Ghana. He also started building a sports academy to unite able-bodied and disabled athletes. "In this world, we are not perfect. We can only do our best," he said. "I just want to make life better and help people benefit from my experience."

One of the people moved by Yeboah's experience and message was Ghana's president at the time, John Kufuor. He used his influence to pass a bill guaranteeing equal rights for disabled people in Ghana.

Yeboah had once been a baby whom almost no one wanted. But through his own determination and the generosity of others, he succeeded in changing attitudes and ideas in his country. A documentary film about his mission was called *Emmanuel's Gift*. Oprah

Winfrey narrated the movie. As she said, it's the story of a man who "had nothing but gave everything and changed a nation forever."

EMMANUEL'S INSPIRATION

In 2005, Emmanuel Ofosu Yeboah received the Arthur Ashe Courage Award. So did a man who had inspired him—Jim MacLaren. MacLaren had been a college football player. In 1985, at the age of 22, MacLaren was in a motorcycle accident. Doctors had to amputate part of his left leg. So MacLaren turned his attention to endurance sports. He became the world's fastest amputee marathoner and triathlete. Eight years later, tragedy struck again. During a triathlon, a van hit MacLaren. This accident left his arms and legs paralyzed. Afterward, a fundraising triathlon in MacLaren's honor raised more money than expected. The remaining funds helped launch the Challenged Athletes Foundation, the organization that made Yeboah's ride possible.

MacLaren died in 2010. Yeboah, whom he had motivated and befriended, said, "I will never forget him in my life."

"GET HER A TEAM"

2005 • EVANSTON, ILLINOIS, UNITED STATES

"This has been such a bad thing," Denis Murphy once said about his daughter Jaclyn's health struggles. "But sometimes good comes out of bad."

A few years earlier, a lacrosse team had been struggling in a totally different way. Something good came out of that, too. The team was the women's lacrosse squad at Northwestern University, near Chicago. Northwestern's squad, the Wildcats, didn't become a varsity team until 2002. Experts expected the group to struggle against more experienced teams from the East Coast. The team needed some great motivation. In 2005, they got it. Northwestern assistant coach Alexis Venechanos heard about a girl from her hometown. Nine-year-old Jaclyn Murphy of Yorktown, New York, was a budding lacrosse player. But she had a form of brain cancer. She had to stop playing the game she loved while she was sick. That's when a team looking for a spark discovered a girl looking for much the same thing.

Venechanos invited Murphy to watch the team when it traveled east for a game. Soon, the Northwestern players rallied around the girl. They

"DON'T EVER GIVE UP"

Jim Valvano was a longtime basketball coach at North Carolina State University. He's best remembered for two moments. The first was in 1983. That's when Valvano's team pulled off a last-second upset to win the NCAA tournament. In his excitement, Valvano ran up and down the court looking for someone to hug! Ten years later, Valvano won the first Arthur Ashe Courage Award. At the time, he was dying of bone cancer. As he accepted the award, he announced the creation of the V Foundation for Cancer Research. The foundation's motto comes from a speech Valvano once gave. That motto is: "Don't Give Up . . . Don't Ever Give Up." Valvano said, "Cancer can take away all of my physical abilities. It cannot touch my mind, it cannot touch my heart, and it cannot touch my soul. And those three things are going to carry on forever." Valvano died only eight weeks later. His foundation carried on. It has since donated more than $90 million to cancer research.

called Murphy to chat and to give her their support. They sent her music to listen to as she recovered from surgery, radiation, and chemotherapy. They even gave her a jersey and named her an honorary Wildcat. "She gave off this incredible energy," said Venechanos. That energy inspired the Wildcats.

Murphy often said she would play lacrosse again when she got well. Meanwhile, the Wildcats played for Murphy. And they played *well.* In fact, the team went undefeated that season. Their record took them all the way to the NCAA championship game. There they faced a favored University of Virginia squad. Murphy was there to watch the game. At halftime, she predicted that her beloved Wildcats would win 13–10. That's exactly what they did. And Murphy was right in the middle of the team's celebration.

"Virginia had more talent at that point," said senior All-American Lindsay Finocchiaro. "But we had heart and motivation." After the game, Finocchiaro gave Murphy her championship watch.

In this unlikely relationship between Murphy and the Wildcats, it was hard to say who got more. Was it the girl who felt like part of a team? Or was it the team that felt part of something much more important than a game?

Murphy soon gave an important gift to others, too. While she was being treated at a hospital, another young patient was in the bed next to her. Murphy's fellow patient marveled at the attention Murphy was getting from the Northwestern players. Murphy later turned to her dad and said, "We have to get her a team."

That was the beginning of the Friends of Jaclyn Foundation. Its mission is to improve the quality of life for kids who have brain tumors. To do this, Friends of Jaclyn pairs young patients with nearby college and high school athletic teams. By May 2008, teams had been matched up with nine children. A year later, 90 children were paired with teams. And now there are more than 300 kids with honorary membership on teams in nearly two dozen sports. The teams range from a softball squad in Nevada to a basketball team in New York.

As for the Northwestern women's lacrosse team, they would go on to win five straight national championships. That was a record-breaking streak. But amid all the victory celebrations, Murphy still inspired the players and coaches. She reminded them that every day you're alive is a victory. "That's the most she's given me," said Finocchiaro. "Live life to the fullest."

KINDHEARTED FATHER

2012 • WASHINGTON, D.C., UNITED STATES

Etan Thomas spent nine seasons in the NBA. Between 2001 and 2011, he played for three different teams. At the same time, he always tried to make a difference off the court. At age 27 he published a collection of poems. The book's title describes Thomas perfectly: *More Than an Athlete*. The 6-foot-9 Thomas has devoted himself to many causes he cares about. His activities have included joining peace rallies and giving speeches during presidential campaigns. He also donated thousands of dollars to relief efforts after an earthquake in Haiti.

But in 2007, at the age of 29, Thomas got frightening news. At a doctor's checkup, Thomas learned that one of his heart valves was leaking. To fix the problem, he needed an operation. It was a scary time.

A year later, Thomas returned to the basketball court. He even recorded 10 points and eight rebounds in his first game back! But he was a different man. The experience had changed his life. "It's something that opens your eyes about everything you have," he said, "and everything you've been able to do."

Thomas's experience also motivated him to take on a very personal project. During his recovery and his time away from basketball, Thomas thought a lot about being a dad. (He and his wife, Nichole, have three children.) He considered the joy and the responsibility of being a father.

Thomas joined President Barack Obama's

Responsible Fatherhood and Healthy Families Task Force. This group works to raise awareness about the impact fathers have in children's lives. Thomas also began talking at schools and also at prisons across the United States. Many

of the people he spoke to were boys and young men from single-parent homes. "I see myself in those kids. There's all this anger inside," said Thomas. "So they make bad choices."

Long ago, Thomas had vowed not to start down the wrong path himself. His parents got divorced when he was seven. After that, Thomas was raised by his mother. She was a schoolteacher. She took him to plays and poetry readings in their home of Harlem, New York. She raised her son to love books and learning. But when Thomas came home from school one day, he found her watching television with tears in her eyes. She was listening to scary statistics about kids who come from single-parent households. "We made a pact," recalled Thomas. "I told her I was going to make right choices."

Thomas worked hard at those choices throughout his life. His dedication and talent helped him succeed in basketball. Outside the game, he worked to help others. That work earned him the 2010 NBA Players Association Community Contribution Award. He also wrote another book. *Fatherhood: Rising to the Ultimate Challenge* was published in 2012. In it, Thomas discussed being a dad. He also described what it was like to grow up mostly without a father around. He included essays that other people wrote on the subject, too. These 44 other writers were athletes, entertainers, and politicians. They included NBA star Kevin Durant, skateboarding legend Tony Hawk, and musician Chuck D.

One of Thomas's goals was to show how important fathers can be. But he also wanted the men who shared their insights in the book to come from all kinds of families. For example, some grew up in two-parent homes. Others didn't. But all achieved success. "We always hear statistics about how if you come from a broken home, you're not going to make it. So now what? Life isn't over!" said Thomas. "It's the situation you have, and you make the most of it."

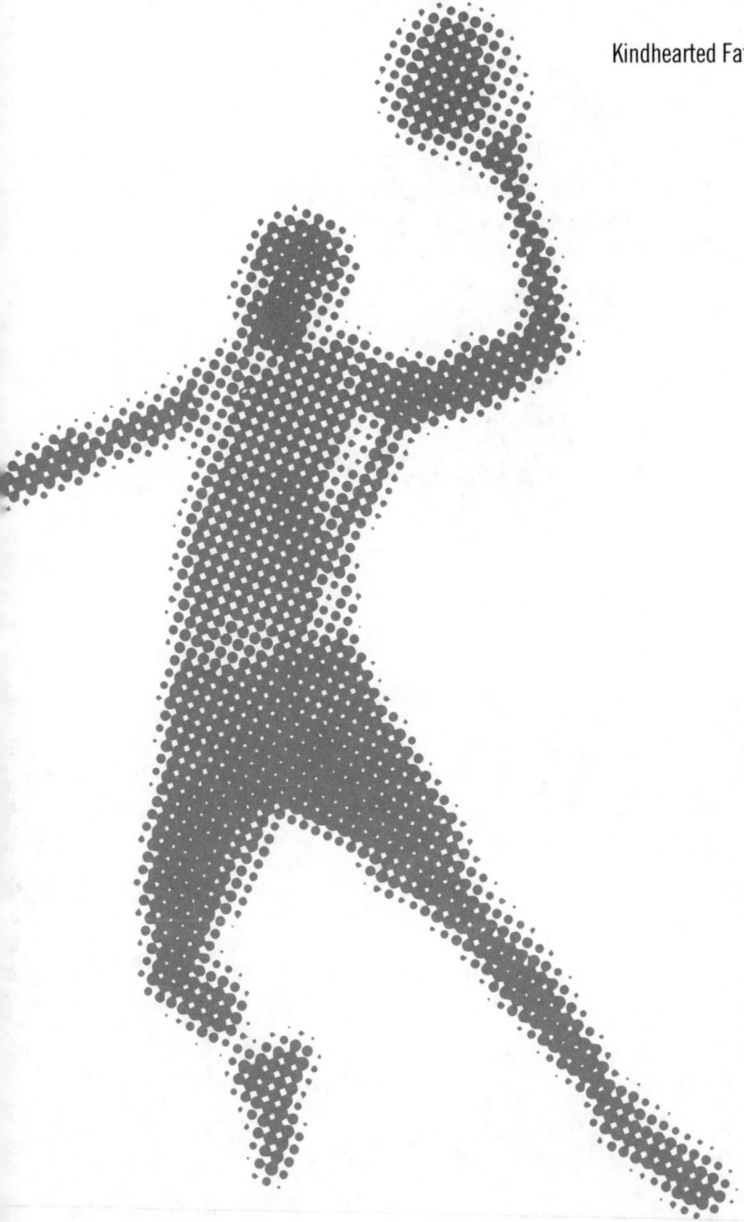

LEAVING A LEGACY

1972 • PUERTO RICO

On the last day of the 1972 baseball season, Roberto Clemente recorded his 3,000th hit. The 38-year-old Pittsburgh Pirates outfielder became only the 11th major leaguer to reach this milestone. He'd led a remarkable career. That career included a .317 lifetime batting average, a National League MVP Award, and a World Series MVP Award. He also had four league batting titles and 12 Gold Glove Awards as the league's best defensive right fielder. But Clemente never could have known that his 3,000th hit would be his last.

Two days before Christmas 1972, a huge earthquake hit Nicaragua. It devastated the capital city of Managua. Clemente had been in the city three weeks earlier for the Amateur Baseball World Series. At that event, Clemente had managed an all-star team from his native Puerto Rico. After the earthquake, he volunteered to help right away. He led the Puerto Rican relief effort to Nicaragua.

This work was only the latest of Clemente's many charitable acts. His other projects included creating free baseball camps and programs for kids. Clemente also dreamed of building a sports complex in Puerto Rico. He wanted young athletes to learn baseball and life skills there. He once said, "If you have a chance to accomplish something that will make things better for someone coming behind you, and you don't do that, you are wasting your time on this earth."

In the week after the earthquake, Clemente raised nearly $150,000. He helped send 26 tons of medicine, food, and clothing to Nicaragua. But he found out that Nicaraguan government officials were stealing many of the supplies. So Clemente decided to make sure the aid would reach the people who needed it. And he decided the best way to do that was to take it to them himself. On New Year's Eve, Clemente climbed into an airplane. The old plane was overloaded with supplies. The flight took off from Puerto Rico just after 9 p.m. Not much later, the plane had engine trouble and crashed into the ocean. Clemente's body was never found.

After Clemente died, many people honored his life and his generosity. Baseball writers immediately elected him to the National Baseball Hall of Fame. He has also been inducted into the World Sports Humanitarian Hall of Fame. In memory of his community and charity work, Clemente was awarded the Congressional Gold Medal and the Presidential Citizens Medal. In addition, Major League Baseball renamed its humanitarian award the Roberto Clemente Award. A statue of Clemente also stands in front of Pittsburgh's PNC Park. Not far away is the Roberto Clemente Bridge. Around the United States, there are also various stadiums and schools named for the player. Baseball commissioner Bud Selig called him "a hero in every sense of the term."

Clemente's actions on and off the field also inspired countless Latin American baseball players—even after he was gone. In fact, his death spurred efforts to make his dream of a Puerto Rican "Sports City" a reality. The local government donated land for the project, and a TV station donated free time for a fundraising telethon. The Pirates offered to play exhibition games to raise money. In addition, Clemente's widowed wife and their son worked tirelessly. Today, Roberto Clemente Sports City is a 304-acre, multi-sport complex. It hosts hundreds of thousands of young athletes each year. So while people sometimes say that Clemente disappeared without a trace, nothing could be further from the truth.

SELECTED BIBLIOGRAPHY

Avila, Oscar. "Francisco Rodriguez: Boxer's Death Grants Chance at Life." *Chicago Tribune*. November 25, 2009.

Belsky, Gary. "Giving Receivers." *ESPN The Magazine*. June 11, 2012.

Dahlgren, Kristen. "Former Olympian Grants Wishes to Seniors." NBC News. *dailynightly.nbcnews.com/_news/2012/04/30/11473610-former-olympian-grants-wishes-to-seniors*. April 30, 2012 (accessed September 22, 2012).

Herzog, Brad. "Breaking the Silence." *Sports Illustrated*. August 24, 1992.

Herzog, Brad. "On, Brief Old Army Team!" *Sports Illustrated*. October 3, 1994.

Huckshorn, Kristin. "Nigerian Basketball Star Gives Back." ESPN. *sports.espn.go.com/espn/otl/columns/story?id=5049920*. April 4, 2010 (accessed August 25, 2012).

Kanamori, Danny. "When Winning Isn't Everything." *columbiasportsjournalism.com/2011/06/14/when-winning-isnt-everything*. June 14, 2011 (accessed October 1, 2012).

Reynolds, Lauren. "'Friends of Jaclyn' Step Up to Raise Funds, Awareness." *sports.espn.go.com/ncaa/news/story?id=2806427*. March 23, 2007 (accessed March 25, 2014).

Rosenberg, Michael. "The Marine and the Orphan." *Sports Illustrated*. August 27, 2012.

Taylor, Phil. "A Cup of Kindness." *Sports Illustrated*. March 19, 2012.

Tierney, Mike. "Wake Forest Baseball Coach Donates Kidney to Player." *The New York Times*. February 9, 2011.

Wertheim, L. Jon. "Why Ask Why?" *Sports Illustrated*. August 20, 2012.

INDEX